Understanding Christmas

An Examination of the Birth of Jesus Christ Using Semitic Bible Study Methods

Michael Harvey Koplitz

ACKNOWLEDGMENTS

This work could not have been accomplished without Dr. Anne Davis, who taught me Ancient Bible (Hebraic) study methods, and my two study partners, Rev. Dr. Robert Cook and Pastor Sandra Koplitz. We know the journey has just started and will last a lifetime. The discovery of the depths of God's Word is awaiting us to find.

Contents

Introduction

This is a study of the narrative of the birth of our Lord and Savior Jesus Christ, which is found in the Gospels of Matthew and Luke. Before starting the presentation, it should be noted that the author is not necessarily in agreement with all the scholarly analysis and material that will be presented. In addition, before reading this work, the reader must come to understand that some theorems presented may provoke some emotions. For example, the author once engaged in a discussion and asked the question, "does it matter if Mary, the mother of Jesus, was a virgin?" This question almost provoked a physical confrontation. Please do not decide to tear up this book rather give the ideas some consideration.

Before you read the presentation, ask yourself, "What are the foundational stones of my faith?" Which narratives of the Bible must be absolutely true for you to maintain your faith? Only you can answer this question. Remember, the Gospel were written thirty to seventy years after the resurrection of Jesus Christ. The narratives most probably were passed to each succeeding generation by the mouth to ear method.

Anyone who has ever played the game telephone knows that the original message that was sent down the line is always different when it reaches the other end. The more persons in the telephone chain, the more the message gets distorted. Could the Gospel narratives have changed a bit as they were passed down through the generations until they were written?

In addition, it is known that there are several versions of the Gospels of Matthew, Mark, Luke and John. Unfortunately, Christianity does not have the original Gospels and the ones we have differ. So, which one is correct? We may never discover.

Therefore, everything presented in this document is up for debate and interpretation. Since we do not have an original document and none of us lived when Jesus was born, then everything is speculative. In Semitic Bible Study Methods, it is important to ask questions of the Scripture and to speculate about the answer. This method was introduced by the sage Hillel, who lived approximately seventy years before the birth of Jesus. Remember to question everything. Questioning everything gave rise to the Rabbinic stories (midrashim) and the legends of the Bible.

Christianity rejected the ways of the Semitic people long ago. When the church did this, they lost the understanding that comes from questioning the Scriptures. Also, the church adopted the Greek way of learning, which essentially stopped the Semitic way of studying the Scripture.

If you have been studying the Scripture as the Church teaches, then you may struggle to question the Scriptures. Questioning the Scripture does not mean that you are rejecting the narratives or rejecting the church's interpretation of the Scriptures. Rather, you are trying to expand your understanding.

In order to discover what the Scripture meant in Jesus' day, the filters and traditions of the Church have to be removed. View the Scripture with open eyes, no filters, no glass, nor anything that gives you a defined definition.

Before you start the journey into the question of Christmas, you will want to read the next chapters. In these chapters, you will discover what Greek learning is and what hebraic learning is. It is important for you to understand the difference.

The main differences between the Greek method and Hebraic method of teaching

Once you are aware of the two teaching styles, you will determine if you are in a class or reading a book, whether the analysis and/or teaching method is in a Greek or Hebraic method. In the Greek method, the instructor is right because of advanced knowledge. In the college situation, it is because the professor has his/her Ph.D. in some area of study, so one assumes that he or she knows everything about the topic. For example, Rodney Dangerfield played the role of a middle-aged man going to college. His

English midterm was to write about Kurt Vonnegut Jr. Since he did not understand any of Vonnegut's books, he hired Vonnegut himself to the write the midterm. When it was returned to him, the English Professor told Dangerfield that whoever wrote the paper knew nothing about Vonnegut. This is an example of the Greek method of teaching. Did the Ph.D. English professor thought she knew more about Vonnegut's writings than Vonnegut did? [1]

---

[1] *Back to School.* Performed by Rodney Dangerfield. Hollywood: CA: Paper Clip Productions, 1986. DVD.

In the Greek teaching method, the professor or the instructor claims to be the authority. If you are attending a Bible study class and the class leader says, "I will teach you the only way to understand this biblical book," consider the implications. This method is common since most seminaries and Bible colleges teach a Greek method of learning, which is the same method the church has been using for centuries.

Hebraic teaching methods are unique. The teacher wants the students to challenge what they hear. It is through questioning that a student can learn. In addition, the teacher wants his/her students to excel to a point where the student becomes the teacher.

It is said that if two rabbis come together to discuss a passage of Scripture, the result will be at least ten different opinions. All points of view are acceptable if biblical evidence can support the points. It is permissible and encouraged for students to have multiple opinions. There is a depth to God's Word, and God wants us to find all His messages that are placed in the Scriptures.

Seeking the meaning of the Scriptures beyond the literal meaning is essential to fully understanding God's Word.[2] The Greek method of learning the Scriptures has prevailed over the centuries. One problem is that people often viewed only the literal interpretation of Scripture as valid, as Martin Luther's "sola literalis" prompted, meaning that only the literal interpretation of Scripture was valid. The Fundamentalist movements of today are based on the literal interpretation of the Scripture. Therefore, they do not believe that God placed any deeper, hidden, or secret meanings in the Word.

---

[2] Davis, Anne Kimball. *The Synoptic Gospels*. MP3. Albuquerque: NM: BibleInteract, 2012.

The students of the Scriptures who learn through Hebraic training and understanding have drawn a different conclusion. The Hebrew language itself leads to different interpretations because of the construction of the language. The Hebraic method of Bible study opens avenues of thought about God's revelations in the Scripture that may have never been considered. A question may be raised about the Scripture being studied for which there may not be an immediate answer. If so, it becomes the responsibility of the learners to uncover the meaning. Also, remember that multiple opinions about the meaning of Scripture are also acceptable if they can be supported by Scripture.

An Understanding of Hebraic Thought in Bible Study

We should start this discussion by asking the question, "Why does a reader of the Bible need to understand Hebraic thought?" When we read or listen to most commentaries about the Bible, we listen to the TV pastors, the famous speakers, or even our local church pastors, who tell us how to understand the Bible, but they rarely mention Hebraic thought.

There is a difference between Greek/Western thought and Hebraic thought. It is amazing how many people, including several educated pastors and seminary professors, think Christianity is a western religion. The origin of Christianity is Hebraic! Jesus was a trained rabbinical Jew who ministered around the Sea of Galilee and Judea doing what rabbis do best – interpreting the Hebrew Scriptures. The original twelve disciples of Jesus Christ were all Jewish. They thought

Jewish, they lived Jewish, their culture was Jewish, and many authors of the New Testament were also Jewish. Hebraic storytelling and parables are contained in the Bible. Whether you examine the Old Testament (which will now be referred to as the Hebrew Scriptures) or the New Testament (which will now be referred to as the Christian Scriptures) you are reading Hebraic documents that were composed of Hebraic thought.

Over the past 1900+ years Christianity has been separated from its mother religion Judaism and has transformed itself into a different religion. The understanding of the Scriptures within most church members today has become a Greek/Western interpretation. When Christianity broke away from Judaism, it lost and forgot its Hebraic roots.[3]

---

[3] Davis, Anne Kimball. *First Century Methods I: Recovering Ancient Methods of Bible Study – Course.* Albuquerque: NM: BibleInteract, 2015.

When a Bible student begins to understand the Hebraic way of thinking the Scriptures will be opened up to a deeper understanding and the blessings God offers to His people will become more abundant. A Hebraic view of the Bible reveals a depth of scriptural perception that is amazing. The richness of Scripture is as deep as God is infinite. A passage of Scripture can be read time and time again. Each time one can receive more of what God is revealing. This is the Hebraic process of understanding that there is a rich depth of revelation that God wants to reveal. Consider the Scripture like an onion. It has numerous layers. As you learn about the outer layer of God's revelation in His Word, God reveals the next layer. This increasing depth of understanding continues for a lifetime. There are an infinite number of insights in the Bible because God is infinite.

Let us start with the basic principles of studying the Scriptures. The first thing is to understand a verse or passage's context.[4] This requires more than just reading the verses before and after the passage being studied. The first seven refer to the history and culture of the people; the last two address the text. The following questions need to be asked:[5]

1. Who is the author?

2. When did the author live?

---

[4] Dye, Diana. *Study to Show Yourself Approved.* Albuquerque: NM: BibleInteract, 2014.

[5] Several question in the list from: Diana Dye. Also from: Boman, Thorleif. *Hebrew Thought Compared with Greek.* Philadelphia: Westminster Press, 1960.

3. What time period is the author writing about?

4. What is the author's point of view?

5. What was the cultural and historical setting at the time the writing was done?

6. Who was the audience the author was writing to?

7. What language was used?

8. What is the plain meaning of the passage?

9. What are the presented details?

·   What details are missing?

Unfortunately, there are many modern Christian authors today who take single verses out of context and use them in narrow ways to prove or disprove their point of view. This is an incorrect method of utilizing God's Word. The context of the Bible must be understood in order to comprehend what God is saying. Answering the questions presented above will help establish the context of the passage.

"What is the inner world of biblical thought? What is the cultural mindset of the authors of Holy Writ? Are we to understand the Bible chiefly through the eyes of Hellenism (Greek/Western thought and culture) or through the eyes of Hebrew thought and culture?"[6] A modern example is when a newspaper article from one city in the U.S. is read in another city. If the

---

[6] Wilson, Marvin R. *Our Father Abraham: Jewish Roots of the Christian Faith*. Grand Rapids, MI: W.B. Eerdmans, 1989. 5.

reader in the other city is not aware of the urban problems of the city, the article is addressing, then the article will be read out of context and its true meaning missed. Understanding the environment of the author is important in understanding what is written.

Paul's letters are a large part of the Christian Scriptures. These letters are interpreted today as Christian documents. However, Paul was a pious Jew. When these letters are viewed as being written by a Messianic Jew the theology of Paul expresses becomes clear. "Paul upheld the goodness of the Jewish tradition of the Bible. Indeed, Paul came to understand the Christian life as patterned after that of Judaism."[7] Paul used Hebraic literary devices in his writings such as midrash, echoes, and chiasms. When reading Paul's letters, care needs to be taken to look for these literary devices because these linguistic tools will give a true interpretation of

---

[7] IBID, p. 8.

what Paul was trying to say.

"If Hebrew thinking is to be characterized, it is obvious first to call it dynamic, vigorous, passionate and sometimes quite explosive in kind; correspondingly Greek thinking is static [harmonic or resting], peaceful and moderate."[8] The Word of God is a dynamic and mighty document. When you read Genesis 1, the creation story, you quickly discover that all of God's

---

[8] Boman, Thorleif. *Hebrew Thought Compared with Greek*. Philadelphia: Westminster Press, 1960. 30.

creation occurred by God speaking it. "And God said…" Black Fire on White Fire is what the sages call the Torah. The Black Fire is the ink that is used to write the words of the Torah and the White Fire is the parchment it is written on.[9] When a Torah scroll is worn out, becoming unusable, a funeral service, with a small casket, is held for the scroll that contains the living Word of God.

---

[9] "Rojtman, Betty. *Black Fire on White Fire: An Essay on Jewish Hermeneutics, from Midrash to Kabbalah*. Berkeley: University of California Press, 1998. 3.

When God speaks, God acts. This concept has been applied to a person's word that must translate into a person's actions. "Hebraically, such a concept of pronouncing a word without following it up with actions makes the word null, void and meaningless."[10] God created the Hebrew language not only so God could communicate with us but also so God's people could communicate with Him. Therefore, Hebrew is a sacred

---

[10] Boman, Thorleif. *Hebrew Thought Compared with Greek.* Philadelphia: Westminster Press, 1960. 24.

language. Around 200 BCE Aramaic became the common language outside the Temple and the Synagogue. It was not until the 20th century that Hebrew was revived as a publicly spoken language.[11] For 2100 years Hebrew was a language spoken only in the synagogue while worshiping God.

Hebraic thought views God to have a personality. For example, God is a

---

[11] Fellman, Jack. *The Revival of a Classical Tongue; Eliezer Ben Yehuda and the Modern Hebrew Language*. The Hague: Mouton, 1973. 7.

loving God. In the Hebrew Scriptures God is described as a warrior, judge, provider and creator. The sacred and secular areas of life for Jews in Yeshua's day were intertwined and everything was in God's domain.[12] Hebraic prayers were then and are today short and to the point. Every aspect of life was celebrated in prayer and thanksgiving to God.

---

[12] Wilson, Marvin R. *Our Father Abraham: Jewish Roots of the Christian Faith*. Grand Rapids, MI: W.B. Eerdmans, 1989.156.

Genesis 5:24 and 6:9 tell us that both Enoch and Noah walked with God. The aim of a Jew is to walk with God. To live a life walking with God requires study of the Torah and obeying every aspect of the Torah, which gives the direction and guidance needed to remain on the way."[13]

Regarding the Scriptures, Hebraic thinking tells us there are no contradictions and certainly no errors

---

[13] IBID. 160.

in the Bible. Narratives that seem to be repetitive are also in the Word for a specific reason. Our task in life is to learn and study the Bible so God's revelation can be revealed to us.

There is no one way to interpret Scripture. The idea of discussion, questioning, and debating the meaning of Scripture is a major part of Hebraic thought in Bible study. In addition, the teacher is not considered having the absolute truth of interpretation. That is reserved for God. We can only stretch, and stretch some more, to uncover an increasing depth of meaning.

An Understanding of Greek Thought in Bible Study

Plato's Academy was the forerunner of the modern university system in existence today.[14] Today's Seminaries and Bible Colleges are part of the modern university system and are using the method Plato and his contemporaries employed to view the universe. This Greek system of learning and understanding is also part of our current education system. Therefore,

---

[14] Howland, Jacob. *Plato and the Talmud*. Cambridge: Cambridge University Press, 2011. 130.

we have been taught that when a teacher, considered an expert in his or her field of study, tells us something, we must accept it without question. When exam time comes, the students are expected to repeat what the teacher has said whether they agree with it.

The same occurs in church when the pastor follows the Greek teaching method he/she was taught in Bible College and/or Seminary. The pastor offers a sermon or Bible study and the people sit passively and are expected to agree with the pastor. There is limited dialogue or discussion allowed because the pastor or the presenter are perceived as correct.

In the Greek mindset hermeneutics is a science, and a science proves one way of viewing the world. "Hermeneutics is the study of the methodological principles of interpretation. To interpret the Bible means to understand the Bible."[15] There is a single answer to every question. Of course, today chaos theory and quantum physics is turning the scientific community somewhat upside down because there can be more than one answer to a question at the subatomic level of matter. Greek thinking is static because once you have interpreted a passage of Scripture you never have to study it again because you already have the answer.

---

[15] Trimm, J. *Hermeneutics: How to Understand the Scripture*. Hurst:Texas: Society for the Advancement of Nazarene Judaism, 2000. 4.

"Thomas Aquinas (1225–1274) lived at a critical juncture of western culture when the arrival of the Aristotelian *corpus* in Latin translation reopened the question of the relation between faith and reason, calling into question the *modus vivendi* that had used for centuries."[16] In simpler words, Aquinas reintroduced the need to study the Scriptures in a Greek manner. Since

---

[16] "Aquinas." In *Stanford Encyclopedia of Philosophy*, 1-5. Stanford, CT: Stanford University, Metaphysics Research Lab., 2004. Accessed August 01, 2016. http://plato.stanford.edu/entries/aquinas/.

hermeneutics is viewed as a science, a specific method can determine the interpretation of Scripture. In this mindset, everything in the Scripture must be explainable. When a passage cannot be explained, then the idea of errors in the Bible emerges. Perhaps there are passages in the Scriptures that God has made so complex that they cannot be easily understood. Instead of digging for a depth of meaning, the Greek thinker often offers a "non-biblical" explanation.

Many of the basic assumptions and methods of the great Greek thinkers were incorporated into Christianity. When the church left its Hebraic roots, the methods of thinking were replaced by Greek methods of thought. Since few Jews were becoming believers in Yeshua, the Hebraic methods of Bible study were lost to Christianity.

The Reformation of the church in the 16th century promoted a restoration of the original meaning to the Scriptures but did not go to the Jewish roots of the faith. So, the Reformers discouraged debate from being a part of understanding Scripture. They did the same thing they accused the Catholic Church leadership of doing. The Reformers developed a new understanding of the Scriptures and only their conclusions were allowed. This can be seen in the Protestant church today through the many confessions of faith statements. Each denomination claims the authority of its own interpretation.

When the ideas of emotion and passion are taken out of the Scriptures. The Scriptures become Greek. What is left is reason and logic. When you take debate and dialogue out of the equation of understanding the Bible, the ability to understand that the Scripture has a depth of interpretation and understanding is removed.

Analyzing Scripture in this Greek

method is like putting God in a box. One size fits all. This is definitely not what God intended for His Word. The Bible is a living document which offers many revelations and depth.

Why is it important that Jesus' earthly father was named Joseph?

To answer this question the two Messiah tradition of Judaism needs to be explored. This prophecy comes from the book of Zechariah. The first verse is:

[9] Rejoice greatly, O daughter of Zion! Shout *in triumph*, O daughter of Jerusalem! Behold, your king is coming to you; He is just and endowed with salvation, Humble, and mounted on a donkey, Even on a colt, the foal of a donkey. (Zech. 9:9 NAU)

The second verse to examine is:

2 For I will gather all the nations against Jerusalem to battle, and the city will be captured, the houses plundered, the women ravished and half of the city exiled, but the rest of the people will not be cut off from the city. 3 Then the LORD will go forth and fight against those nations, as when He fights on a day of battle. (Zech. 14:2-3 NAU)

"So the question is, does this king who reigns over all the earth come gently, riding on a donkey in peace? Or in great wrath, ready to do battle? Is Zechariah contradicting himself? This is a big puzzle for Jewish scholars as well. But this is not the only place in the Scriptures where we find seemingly divergent pictures of Messiah"[17]

A Jewish tradition is that God will send two Messiahs. As shown in the book of Zechariah there are two Messiahs, two kings. In chapter nine the King, the Messiah, is described as the one who is humble and is endowed with salvation. Since Jesus entered the city of Jerusalem mounted on a donkey that

---

[17] "The Returning King: The Two Messiahs" in Zechariah"." Jews for Jesus. June 06, 2017. Accessed October 08, 2017. https://jewsforjesus.org/publications/issues/issues-v15-n05/the-returning-king-the-two-messiahs-in-zechariah/.

could make Him the first of the two Messiahs.

The first Messiah was Messiah ben Joseph[18]. His task was to start a spiritual revolution. Jesus is the Messiah ben Joseph. He told us that He came to establish the Kingdom of God/Heaven on Earth. He did not come to start an armed revolution as many of the people thought. The task of the armed revolution is placed in the hands of the second Messiah, Messiah ben David. The book of the Revelation

---

[18] *ben* means "son." Messiah ben Joseph means Messiah son of Joseph

speaks about the return of the Lord Jesus as Messiah ben David.

In the Gospel of Matthew and Luke, Jesus' earthly father is named Joseph. Therefore, Jesus is Messiah ben Joseph. There are some interpretations that the reason for two Messiahs is that there were two Kingdoms of Israel. Messiah ben Joseph is from the tribe of Joseph, more specifically the clan of Ephriam, which was a part of the Northern Kingdom. Messiah ben David is from the Southern Kingdom since David was a King in the Southern Kingdom.

[6] Jacob was the father of Joseph the

husband of Mary, by whom Jesus was born, who is called the Messiah. (Matt. 1:16 NAU)

[23] When He began His ministry, Jesus Himself was about thirty years of age, being, as was supposed, the son of Joseph, the son of Eli (Lk. 3:23 NAU)

Therefore, Jesus' father's name is Joseph because Jesus is Messiah ben Joseph.

Why Bethlehem?

Now after Jesus was born in Bethlehem of Judea (Matt. 2:1 NAU)

So why was it important that Jesus was born in Bethlehem? The Gospel of Mark and John do not mention the birth of Jesus. To those authors, the place of His birth is not important. In Matthew's Gospel, it is more of a passing statement. From the Gospel of Luke:

[1]Now in those days a decree went out from Caesar Augustus, that a census be taken of all the inhabited earth. [2] This was the first census taken while

Quirinius was governor of Syria. [3] And everyone was on his way to register for the census, each to his own city. [4] Joseph also went up from Galilee, from the city of Nazareth, to Judea, to the city of David which is called Bethlehem, because he was of the house and family of David, [5] in order to register along with Mary, who was engaged to him, and was with child. (Lk. 2:1-5 NAU)

The Gospel of Luke created the idea of a census that was ordered by the Roman government. There are no documents outside of the Gospel of Luke to support this idea. Also, if the people had to return to their ancestral home, that would have caused a problem in the Galilee. The Galilee was the territory of Naphtali and Zebulun. The land of these two tribes was in the Northern Kingdom. The Hebrews who lived in the Galilee when Jesus was born would have been from the south, Judea or Benjamin. Therefore, if such a census was declared, practically all the Hebrew people in the Galilee would have to go south. Logistically, that probably could not have happened.

The cities of Judea could not handle the huge number of people who would have had to go there. Jerusalem would not have been able to handle such an influx. Therefore, logic says that this census order probably was not given.

Semitic stories are extremely colorful. The imagery presented in the stories of the Hebrew Scriptures and in the Gospels is some of the best ever written. The author of Luke's Gospel believed Jesus had to be born in Bethlehem, therefore he created a need for Mary and Joseph to journey to the south.

4 Joseph also went up from Galilee, from the city of Nazareth, to Judea, to the city of David which is called

Bethlehem, because he was of the house and family of David, [5] in order to register along with Mary, who was engaged to him, and was with child. (Lk. 2:4-5 NAU)

In the Gospel of Luke, the author refers to the city of David as Bethlehem. "The city of Jerusalem was originally built around the Gihon Spring, on the southeastern hill to the south (left) of the Temple Mount, which is today crowned with the gold-domed Dome of the Rock. Jerusalem has been continuously inhabited since at least 3000 BC, but it was only in the time of Solomon that the city limits expanded beyond the southeastern spur, known today as the "City of David."[19] The City of David is not Bethlehem but the south of Jerusalem. By Jesus' day the city of David had been absorbed into Jerusalem.

2 "But as for you, Bethlehem Ephrathah, *Too* little to be among the clans of Judah, From you One will go forth for Me to be ruler in Israel. His goings forth are from long ago, From the days of eternity." (Mic. 5:2 NAU)

---

[19] "Jerusalem, City of David and Area G (BiblePlaces.com)." BiblePlaces.com. Accessed October 08, 2017. (Jerusalem's City of David and Area G, 2017)

This prophecy from the book of Micah has been interpreted that the Messiah will be born in Bethlehem. Which Messiah was born, Ben Joseph or Ben David? If Jesus is Messiah ben Joseph, as shown earlier, then He should have been born in the Galilee. Messiah ben Joseph is to be from the Northern Kingdom (this is probably another reason that Jesus had come from Nazareth). Bethlehem is a city that was in Judea, in the Southern Kingdom.

Is it possible that the Gospel writers got this wrong? Since the church wanted to separate itself from Judaism, then the knowledge of the two

Messiahs might not have been known. It is Messiah ben David who will be born in Bethlehem or somewhere in the territory of the old Southern Kingdom.

This might explain why Jesus' mission was misunderstood. If His disciples saw Him as Messiah ben David, they would have expected the armed revolution. Near the end of Jesus' life, they understood that Jesus was Messiah ben Joseph.

So, if Jesus is Messiah ben Joseph, then he was not supposed to be born in the south. Perhaps the authors of Mark's and John's Gospel realized Jesus was Messiah ben Joseph and included nothing about His birth. By not speaking about the place of His birth, they avoided the complication of the two Messiahs. For prophecy's sake Jesus had to be born in Bethlehem because the people believed that Messiah ben David had come.

Did Mary have to be a virgin?

As I mentioned in the introduction, this can be a touchy question. The Apostle's Creed and Nicene Creed say that Jesus was born of the virgin Mary. The early Gentile Christian church believed this. Scientifically, can a virgin birth occur?

"Parthenogenetic reproduction could occur among human females yet remain unnoticed. Indeed, such a woman could have a husband and be totally unaware of her own condition. She would have only daughters, each of which would carry only her genes, which would almost certainly increase in the gene pool, at least over the short term. Is there any evidence for this? Claims of reproduction without males are not to be expected from nunneries, but neither have any emanated from prisons where women are kept isolated from men. Parthenogenesis in humans may seem far-fetched, but 50 years ago no-one suspected that parthenogenesis could occur in any vertebrate: now all-female species have been documented in fish, amphibians, reptiles and birds (all major orders of vertebrates except mammals).[20]

---

[20] Virgin Birth in Human Females? [Copyright, Eric R. Pianka]. Accessed October 09, 2017.

A virgin birth is possible biologically, however the offspring of a virgin birth must be a female. The Y chromosome needed to produce a male would be missing. The ovum would have to have two strains of DNA and each would contain the X chromosome.

Throughout history there have been virgin births. "Virgins have given birth to the godheads of nearly every major religion. It's a particular motherhood: these mythical virgins never give birth

---

http://www.zo.utexas.edu/courses/thoc/virginbirth.html.

to other women."[21]

From Hebraic mysticism the body, soul and spirit are defined as:

Nefesh – this is the flesh, blood and bones which exist in the spiritual world of Asiyah.[22] The life force from God is blown into the body (like God did to Adam). This is the part of humans that goes to the grave, the body.

Ruach – this part of the spirit

---

[21] Edwards, Stassa. "The History of Virgin Births." Jezebel. December 24, 2014. Accessed October 09, 2017. https://jezebel.com/the-history-of-virgin-births-1674159265.
[22] Asiyah is the spiritual world kof action as defined in the Kabbalah. This is the world we leave in.

develops in the world of Yetzirah.[23] This is our personal thoughts and emotions, our ability to love, our ability to recognize God. This is our intellect and the ability to love God with all your soul. This is our personality.

Neshamah – God's spark in each of us which originates in the spiritual world Atzilut.[24] It is this God spark which

---

[23] Yetzirah is the spiritual world in the Kabbalah and is the spiritual of formation.
[24] Atzilut is the spiritual world in the Kabbalah of emanation.

gives us life.

For the Messiah Jesus His Ruach and Neshamah were God. His nefesh had to be of this Earth. Since the essence of who we are is placed into our nefesh (our flesh) and that makes us who we are. How much does it matter how the nefesh that Jesus occupied on Earth was created?

From the Hebraic point of view it does not matter. It is the ruach and neshamah that matters. However, for the early church which was creating a new religion at the time, it was important to be able to set its roots in antiquity. That is one reasons why the Hebrew Scriptures were important to the early church. By basing Christianity in the antiquity of the Hebrew Scriptures the new religion would be accepted by the people.

The major religions of the ancient world, except for Judaism, had their god created from a virgin birth. From antiquity we find, "But the cultural longing for a virgin birth is not the sole domain of Christianity. In Egypt, Queen Mautmes was visited by the ibis-headed Thoth, the messenger of the gods, and told that she would soon bear a son although she was a virgin.

Mautmes's virgin pregnancy was so revered that celebratory scenes were carved on the walls of Luxor Temple. There, she is escorted by both the holy spirit Kneph and the goddess Hathor to a cross symbolizing life; in the following scenes, she gives birth and her son Amen-hetep is enthroned. At his feet he receives the gifts of three men; he was worshiped."[25]

"And there is Hera, queen of Olympus, who renewed her virginity every year in the holy waters of Kanathos. She

---

[25] Edwards, Stassa. "The History of Virgin Births." Jezebel. December 24, 2014. Accessed October 09, 2017. https://jezebel.com/the-history-of-virgin-births-1674159265.

spurned her adulterous husband (and the attention of mortal men), holding tightly to the moral authority that her virginity granted her. Hera scarified sex; in return she was rewarded with a son.

There is also Kausalya, the virgin mother of Rama, an avatar of Vishnu. There's the venerated Queen Maya of Nepal who, during a vision, was visited by a white elephant carrying a lotus in his trunk. The white elephant walked into her womb and reemerged on earth as the Buddha.

Virgins have given birth to the godheads of nearly every major religion. But it's a particular kind of motherhood: these mythical virgins never give birth to other women, and in the rare cases when they give birth to mortals, the men are far from ordinary. Genghis Khan was born to a virgin, stories say, as was Plato: he, according to Diogenes Laertius, was the son of Apollo."[26]

There are additional stories from antiquity of virgin births. Jesus had to have a virgin birth. In the time of Jesus' birth the Mithras religion was popular in the Roman Empire. "The ancient mythological deity worshipped in Persia

---

[26] IBID.

four hundred years prior to Jesus (and worshipped continually throughout the first four or five centuries of these millennium in Rome, right alongside those who worshipped Jesus). Jesus "mythers" claim Mithras was born of a virgin, in a cave, on December 25th, and his birth was attended by shepherds."[27]

Besides being of a virgin birth, Mithras was born in a cave (just like Jesus being born in a manger), and he was born on December 25th. It is possible that when

---

[27] Jwallace. "Is Jesus Simply a Retelling of the Mithras Mythology?" Cold Case Christianity. May 05, 2014. Accessed October 09, 2017. http://coldcasechristianity.com/2014/is-jesus-simply-a-retelling-of-the-mithras-mythology/.

Paul created his churches that he took the Mithras cult, changed the deity to Jesus of Nazareth, and removed some of the extreme pagan rituals.

Using this theory, it was important that Jesus was born of a virgin, in a cave, and eventually the Roman Empire decided Jesus was born on December 25th. In the Gnostic Gospels the birth of Jesus is not mentioned, nor is the idea that His mother Mary was a virgin.

The question for the reader is, does it matter if Mary was a virgin or not when Jesus was born? Since tradition has been a driving factor in the church for

1900 years the church would say absolutely.

Spiritually it would not matter since the virgin birth deals with the nefesh. It is not the nefesh that made Jesus the Messiah and God incarnate. It was Jesus' ruach and neshamah which was God and thus made Him God on Earth.

In the long run does it matter if believers in Jesus believe that Mary was a virgin or not? Not really because either way Jesus was God on Earth.

The Three Wise Men and the Trip to Egypt

^{1} Now after Jesus was born in Bethlehem of Judea in the days of Herod the king, magi from the east arrived in Jerusalem, saying, ^{2} "Where is He who has been born King of the Jews? For we saw His star in the east and have come to worship Him." (Matt. 2:1-2 NAU)

The term "magi" refers to astrologers from the territory of Persia. The prophecies of the Hebrew Scriptures were well known throughout the world in Jesus' day. Undoubtedly, these three magi must have been studying the book of Isaiah. When they saw the Star of

Bethlehem in the eastern sky they believed that the Hebrew Messiah had to be born.

Referring to the prophecy of Micah 5:2, the magi went to Bethlehem to see the baby Jesus. Matthew's Gospel does not say how long after Jesus' birth that the three magi came to Bethlehem. From the Gospel, we know that their arrival caused quite a stir. King Herod was obsessed with destroying anyone who could take his throne away from him.

The Gospel of Matthew then continues to tell the tale of Joseph taking the family to Egypt. The magi and the story of Egypt are only found in Matthew's Gospel. The author wanted to include as numerous prophecies about the birth of the Messiah Jesus as they could. The trip to Egypt comes from Hosea.

When Israel *was* a youth I loved him,
And out of Egypt I called My son.
(Hos. 11:1 NAU)

Would Herod have stopped his search for the baby Jesus? His fear of being overthrown would have irritated him until he captured Jesus and had Him killed. So, did this story occur?

Matthew's Gospel has a thread that Jesus is the replacement for the Law Giver, Moses. Moses, as an infant, faced death and was saved. Jesus as an infant, faced death and was saved. Jesus was not placed on the Nile River, however, both Jesus and Moses were in Egypt when their early lives were threatened. This is just one of the numerous parallels between Jesus' and Moses' lives.

If the event of the magi occurred, then Jesus would have been known to the world. He would not have been able to grow up as a human child because he would have received constant attention.

In John's Gospel, the story of the wedding at Cana, Jesus tells His mother Mary that it was not His time. What that means is that Jesus was not ready to be introduced to the world.

If Jesus was not ready as an adult to become known to the world at Cana, then certainly He was not ready to be introduced to the world as an infant.

Michael H. Koplitz

The Angels of Luke's Gospel

The story of Jesus' birth from Luke's Gospel is a beautiful story. The evening Jesus was born, angels went out into the fields to tell the shepherds go see the event. As with other birth events in the Gospel of Matthew, this narrative only appears in the Gospel.

The problem with the story is that Jesus would have become well known. People would come from all over the Empire just to see Him. The same argument about it not being Jesus' time from the magi story applies here.

In order for Jesus to grow up like a normal child, his birth had to be kept a secret. People would have come from all over the world to see the child and to request Him to perform miracles.

Semitic Story Telling

Story telling is a way God wanted the Scriptures to be written, so He blessed the authors of Scriptures with the ability to tell stories. Semitic story telling is concerned about the essential message of the story. The details are far from important.

For example, in each of the four Gospels, you will find four different stories about Jesus' resurrection. Using Greek/Western thinking, the reader would say that these stories conflict with each other.

However, in Semitic story telling the

details of the story is not important. To understand the Holy Scriptures, it is important to be using Ancient Bible study methods, thus approaching the stories as the Hebrew people did 2000 years ago.

The Gospel stories of Jesus' resurrection seem different from the Greek/Western eye. To the Hebraic eye, they are the same. The meaning of the four stories is that the tomb of Jesus was empty and He had arisen from the grave. That is all that matters.

So, when we look at the stories about the birth of Jesus, it does not matter what the details are. The stories of

Matthew and Luke tell us the same thing. Jesus Christ was born as an infant. When it happened or how it happened, or what else transpired because of His birth does not matter. These are stories that are of Hebraic origin.

The more colorful the story is, the easier it is for people to remember the story. It is possible that the stories about Jesus' birth grew as the years passed between Jesus' resurrection and the writing of the Gospels. Semitic story tellers probably added their own signatures to the stories.

Whether the stories of Christmas are

factual does not matter, that Jesus was born like us is.

Conclusion

Christmas is a wonderful time of the year when the believers and disciples of Jesus Christ come together to celebrate the birth of the Messiah of the world. So much pageantry goes into the celebration and it is a great time of the year. The world gets to see that Christians can come together and love each other. What would be better is if the Christians of the world could keep the Christmas spirit throughout the year.

At the beginning of this book, you were asked about how many of the

Bible stories have to be true for your faith. Here at the end, it is hoped that your eyes are opened not only about the stories of Christmas but also the rest of the stories of the Bible.

The details of the stories are not as critical as the meaning of the story. From a scholarly perspective, when utilizing Ancient Bible study methods, the narratives surrounding Christmas fulfill prophecy but are lacking in probability. The next step for the reader would be to look at the spiritual implications of the Christmas stories. If you look at the stories not only as Semitic stories but also as stories written by theologians, then the details of each story exist to bring us closer to our God and our Lord and Savior Jesus Christ.